The Most Incredible Science Experiment Book Ever!

Mad Marc (Wileman)

ISBN 978-1-291-73612-0

'The Most Incredible Science Experiment Book Ever' is the book I wish had been available when I was a kid!

Let's get started!

CONTENTS:

The Intro Stuff:

The Most Incredible Experiments:

WARNING: (legal type stuff)

WARNING No 1:
You and your child may get excited about science!

WARNING No 2:
All these experiments are reasonably low risk however things can (and will) sometimes go wrong! Please follow the instructions carefully, make sure you have an adult on hand to help out and note that I or Sublime Science expressly disclaim all liability for any occurrence, including, but not limited to, damage, injury or death which might arise as consequences of the use of any experiment(s) listed or described here. Therefore, you assume all the liability and use these science experiment projects at your own risk!

Mad Marc Says:
Have Fun! Get a sane and sensible adult to help you - but get stuck in - have a go and enjoy doing it!

INTRODUCTION:

What's it all about?

In short - This is the book that I dreamt about when I was a kid! A 'how to' guide of awesome experiments that you can do with stuff that you've already got!

Who wrote this thing?

Hi! I'm Mad Marc (Marc Wileman on more sensible occasions!) and I founded Sublime Science to show children just how awesome science can be! I've got a First Class Masters Degree in Physics (Universities of Nottingham & Toronto) and have been a Professional Science Communicator (maker of slime & launcher of rockets!) across the UK, Canada and Australia too!

I'm proud to have been featured by the BBC, ITV & The Telegraph and to have worked with the British Science Association and National Science Museum. I've even received a congratulatory letter from 10 Downing Street! - Enough about me - Let's get started!

1. The Naked Egg Experiment!

This could well be my favourite eggsperiment ever, and not just for the chance to make egg jokes. EVERY child should make a naked egg, it's absolutely incredible! (No more egg jokes, I promise!)

What do I need:
- A glass
- An egg
- White vinegar
- Lots of patience! (Harder to find than eggs and vinegar!)

How do I do it?

STEP1 - Fill your glass full enough with white vinegar so that you can completely cover your egg.

STEP2 - Pop your egg in and

look closely! See all of those bubbles on the surface - that's what's going to get our egg naked!

STEP3 - Wait...

STEP4 - Keep waiting...Only kidding! But to get your egg entirely naked will take at least 24 hours! It's well worth the wait though, I promise!

STEP5 - Gently! Bounce your naked egg, yes, you read that correctly! Naked eggs bounce! Too much fun. Get started, right away! And remember to come back and read about how it all works too!

What's going on?

Why does vinegar get our egg naked? Well, the first clue is those little bubbles that you can see! Those bubbles mean there's a chemical reaction going on! The shell of an egg is made of calcium carbonate ($CaCO_3$). This reacts with the acid of the vinegar and causes bubbles of carbon dioxide to be given off. Eventually your whole eggshell will have been turned into carbon dioxide gas!

Luckily, under the hard outer shell of your egg is a membrane. You can see through the membrane and even see the yolk moving around. Oh, and naked eggs bounce too!

WARNING: This is addictive and if you bounce it too hard you'll need to start over with a new egg! Oh, don't eat your egg! It's basically been pickled in vinegar!

More Fun Please - Experiment like a real scientist!
- Does it have to be vinegar that you use, what other safe things could you try?
- How high can you bounce your egg before it goes splat?
- How long will your egg last for?

2. How to Make a Hovercraft

Hovercrafts are absolutely brilliant and definitely a huge amount of fun - now's the time to make your own. You won't be able to sit on it and ride around but you will be able to have a huge amount of fun watching it glide across your desk! You'll learn a thing or two about friction too!

What do I need?
- Water bottle top
- Blue-Tac
- Balloon
- CD or DVD (that you don't mind if it gets scratched)

How do I do it?

STEP1 - Roll the Blue-Tac into a sausage shape and press it down onto the CD, in a circle around the

the hole. Push the bottle top down onto the Blue-Tac so that it sticks to the CD with no gaps for the air to escape.

STEP2 - Blow up the balloon pretty full and then twist the bottom round several times (so the air doesn't all come out while you're attaching it to your hovercraft base!)

STEP3 - Let's take your hovercraft for a test drive! Stretch the balloon over the bottle top, untwist the balloon and you're off. Try pushing your hovercraft gently and watch how far it glides across your desk!

What's going on?

Why do hovercrafts glide so effortlessly? It all has to do with friction, or lack of it! As the air comes out of the balloon it spreads out under the CD so the hovercraft isn't actually touching the table but floating just above it on a cushion of air!

WARNING: Don't do this experiment if you need to be somewhere, it's impossible to resist the temptation to have another go - it was for me anyway!

More Fun Please - Experiment like a real scientist!

- Try adding weight to your hovercraft, maybe more Blue-Tac, how does that change things?
- What about blowing the balloon up more, or less?
- Can you find a way to extend your hovercraft, make the base even bigger, how does that change things?
- Does it work on different surfaces? How come?!

3. The Invincible Balloon

When a balloon goes up against a candle there seems like there can only be one winner! Think again, here's how to make your balloon invincible and learn a thing or two about conductivity too!

What do I need:
- Candle
- Matches
- Balloon (or two!)

How do I do it?

STEP1 - Make sure you've got an adult to help out. The first step is to light the candle. Then inflate your balloon. If you want to prove what you know will happen you can try lowering your balloon over the flame.

WARNING: Your balloon will pretty quickly go pop!

STEP2 - Let's make the balloon invincible. Fill your balloon up with water, then inflate it. This means there'll be a small puddle of water in the bottom of the balloon.

STEP3 - Slowly lower your balloon down on top of the flame of the candle. Hold it there, does it go pop? You can lower it right down and actually put the candle out with the balloon. Finally, make sure to have a look at the bottom of the balloon.

What's going on?

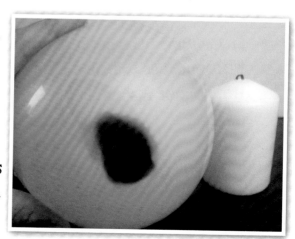

Well, why does the balloon go pop when there is no water inside it? It's really just the heat from the candle

13

melting the outside of the balloon untill it's so weak that it can't contain the pressure of the air that's inside of it!

How does the water make a difference? That puddle of water inside of the balloon pulls the heat away from the surface of the balloon. This is called conduction. So, instead of the balloon skin getting so hot it melts, the heat is spread (or 'dissipated') into the water that's inside the balloon. That water slowly starts to get warmer but the balloon doesn't pop.

More Fun Please - Experiment like a real scientist!

- Try adding different amounts of water to the balloon, does that make a difference?
- How about if you blow the balloon up really full of air?

4. How To Make A Paper Helicopter

Paper aeroplanes are great and a great way to learn about science but they've got nothing on paper helicopters, that's for sure! All you'll need is some paper, scissors and maybe a paperclip!

What do I need:

- A piece of paper
- Some scissors
- A paperclip

How do I do it?

STEP1 - The perfect size to make your helicopter is 1/8th of a piece of paper. Great news as you can make 8 of them out of one sheet of A4 paper! Fold your paper into eights and cut one out ready.

STEP2 - I've marked on the image how to make it! Just make a cut where you see a solid line and make a fold where you see a dashed line!

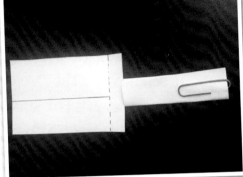

STEP3 - Make the two small cuts and fold the paper over and use a paperclip to hold it in place, as shown.

STEP4 - To make the wings, simply make the cut down the middle solid line and fold the wings down so you've got something that looks like our final helicopter!

STEP5 - No pre-flight checks needed! Simply hold the helicopter up high and drop it! Watch how it spins! If you're feeling brave you can try throwing it but pretty soon you might need to make another helicopter!

16

What's going on?

As your helicopter starts to fall the air pushes past the wings. Most of this air pushes upwards against the falling helicopter (which is why it falls slowly) but each wing causes some of that air to push to the side. There's an equal sideways push on each of the wings but in opposite directions and that's what causes the helipcopter to spin!

More Fun Please - Experiment like a real scientist!

- What happens if you add more weight? Blue Tac is great for this!
- What are the perfect proportions to make your helicopter spin as fast as possible?
- How big a helicopter can you make?

5. The Mysterious Floating Egg

There's something magical about this experiment. You'll have to have a go and try it to believe it's not been faked! Luckily, you'll almost certainly have everything you need waiting for you in your kitchen.

What do I need:
- Egg
- Clear glass
- Salt
- Teaspoon

How do I do it?

STEP1 - Half fill your glass with water and gently lower the egg in.

WARNING: It will sink so be careful otherwise you'll be needing another egg! So now we know that the egg sinks, take it back out again (use your teaspoon to scoop it back out).

STEP2 - Half fill your glass with water and add around 10 teaspoons of salt to it. Don't worry, you can't add 'too much' salt as we're making a 'saturated solution' - that really just means that the water is 'full' of salt, so any extra you add will just sit at the bottom of the glass. Pop your egg in and watch it float, pretty cool, huh!

STEP3 - To make it look really magical, very slowly and carefully pour some tap water on top of your floating egg (you have to be very gentle so the fresh water doesn't mix with the salt water). You now have a floating egg!

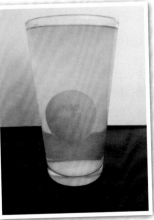

STEP4 - To really see what's going on try gently adding some food colouring to your glass and watch what happens! Only the top half of the glass gets coloured, why is that?

What's going on?

It's all to do with density. The egg is slightly more dense that tap water (so it sinks initially) but less dense than the salt water (so it floats on top of that). The reason we're able to put the egg in the middle of the glass is, as long as we're careful, the less dense tap water sits on top of the more dense salt water and they don't mix together.

More Fun Please - Experiment like a real scientist!
- Does it have to be an egg that you use?
- What other objects could you try?

6. The Exploding Sandwich Bag

Next time you're getting ready to make your lunch, you can dive into a superfun science experiment! This one involves an explosion (only a little one!) and is a great way to learn about chemical reactions too!

What do I need:

- White vinegar
- Bicarbonate of soda or baking soda
- Tissue paper
- A sealable sandwich bag

How do I do it?

STEP1 - Wrap a couple of teaspoons of bicarbonate of soda up inside a tissue, as shown. (This is just to make it easier to get your sandwich bag closed before your chemical reaction gets started!)

WARNING: Make sure to do this experiment outside! (or somewhere that you don't mind making a mess!)

STEP2 - Pour some white vinegar into your sandwich bag until there's around a 3cm layer in the bottom of the bag.

STEP3 - Pop your bicarbonate of soda package inside your bag and hold it above the vinegar while you seal it up!

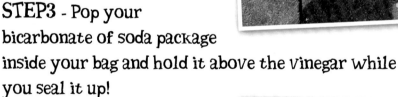

STEP4 - Drop your bicarb down into the vinegar and stand back! Your sandwich bag is getting set to explode! You'll see your bag slowly start to swell up as the pressure builds and then finally...pop!

What's going on?

This is all to do with the pressure being caused by the chemical reaction! As the bicarbonate of soda and the vinegar mix together they react and carbon dioxide is given off. The bag fills with more and more carbon dioxide and soon the pressure will be too much for the bag to take and BOOM! You'll get a beautiful little explosion, perfect!

More Fun Please - Experiment like a real scientist!

- How can you make the bag explode more quickly?
- What happens if you add more vinegar or more bicarbonate of soda?
- What combination produces the biggest explosion?!

7. Scientific Suction!

I love this experiment! It really has to be seen to be believed. Let's get cracking with some scientific suction!

What do I need:

- A plate
- A water bottle
- Some food colouring (optional but cool!)
- Blue Tac
- Matches

How do I do it?

STEP1 - First pour a thin layer of water onto your plate (It's a really cool addition to dye this with some food colouring if you've got it!)

STEP2 - Next up - build yourself a match tower! Roll a blob of Blue Tac into a cylinder shape and then stab 5 matches into the top so you have a match tower (as shown!).

STEP3 - Light your match tower and quickly pop your water bottle over the top! The water will get 'sucked' up into the bottle and this will leave the plate almost dry!

What's going on?

The wrong explanation for this experiment is given out all over the place. People describing the air as being "eaten"! No no no!

Here's what's happening! As you put the bottle over the flame the air inside the bottle starts to heat up. As it gets hotter and hotter that air expands and you'll see some of it bubbles out! Then the oxygen runs out and so the flames go out. The air inside the bottle cools down and gets smaller and the water is actually 'pushed' into the bottle by the 'normal' air pressure in the room!

More Fun Please - Experiment like a real scientist!

- How does changing the number of matches change the experiment?
- How can you change the experiment to suck up the most water possible?

8. Bridge Over Untroubled Water!

There's a touch of magic to this science experiment (and a very cheesy name!). How to get the water from one glass to the other, without touching it? Use science, of course!

What do I need:

- Two glasses
- Toilet roll
- Food colouring (optional)

How do I do it?

STEP1 - I love to start this experiment by asking: "how can you get the water from one glass to the other - without touching either glass?"

STEP2 - Here's the 'trick'. Tear off roughly a one metre long strip of toilet roll then fold and roll it until you get a sausage shape, as shown over the page.

STEP3 - Carefully put it into the glasses as shown. You didn't touch the glasses so this counts!

STEP4 - Watch as the water slowly rises up and swaps between the glasses! This will take a little while so don't sit and watch the whole thing! (The food colouring is just so you can see what's happening and so it looks extra awesome!)

What's going on?

If you've been paying close attention (you have, right!) you'll have noticed that only around half the water has made it across! When you put the toilet paper in the water it started to absorb the water. The absorption ('sucking up') of the toilet roll was stronger than gravity so slowly the water gets pulled up the toilet roll until it gets to the top. From that point on, gravity is helping out and pulls the water down and into the other glass.

So how come all the water doesn't make it across? Well, once there is some water in the previously empty cup the same thing can happen in reverse! That water could be absorbed back to the other side so when there's an equal amount of water in each cup we say that it's reached 'equilibrium'!

More Fun Please - Experiment like a real scientist!

- What difference does adding no food colouring make? Why?
- How tall a glass would this work on? Give it a go!

9. How To Suck Up An Egg!

This experiment is absolutely awesome and a great way to learn a little bit about pressure too! It's just one of those things that you wouldn't believe is possible so you've got to give it a go!

What do I need:
- An egg or 2
- Plastic bottle
- 2 plates or bowls
- Teaspoon
- Food Colouring (optional)

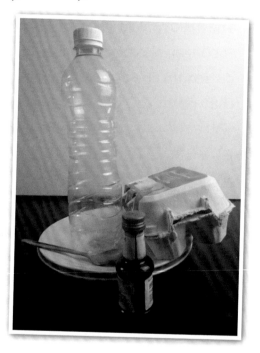

How do I do it?

STEP1 - Break an egg carefully over a plate so the yolk and white stay separated!

STEP2 - We're going to use the plastic bottle to pick up the yolk! Squeeze some air out of the bottle...

...then lower it down until it's touching the yolk. Gently release your squeeze and this will lift the yolk up. Lift the yolk up and put it on the other plate (this may take you a couple of tries!)

STEP3 - This next bit is just for fun, really! Mix in some food colouring with your egg white, this will look a little bit disgusting!

STEP4 - Use the bottle to add the yolk back in (to your coloured egg white) and you'll have a slightly disgusting looking eggy mess!

What's going on?

It's all to do with air pressure!

When you squeeze the bottle initially you push some of the air out. When you put the

bottle top over the yolk this seals the remaining air in. As you release your grip the bottle expands and returns to its normal size but no more air can rush in, as the yolk is in the way. This means you've got the same amount of air in a bigger space so the pressure will be lower. As the pressure outside of the bottle is higher, it's this higher air pressure that pushes the yolk into the bottle!

More Fun Please!
- This is a great experiment to learn about air pressure, what else can you pick up with your bottle?

10. An Indestructible Sandwich Bag?

Next time you're making your packed lunch take an extra couple of minutes and have a go at this outstanding science experiment! All you'll need is an extra sandwich bag (this one won't be any use to you by the time you're done!) and a couple of spare pens!

What do I need:

- A sealable sandwich bag
- Several pens or pencils (they don't have to be matching!)

How do I do it?

STEP1 - Fill your sandwich bag around three quarters of the way full with water and seal the bag!

STEP2 - Push your first pen through your (water-filled) sandwich bag and out the other side. As long as you do this slowly and gently then you should have managed to stay dry!

STEP3 - Just to prove it wasn't a fluke and to make your experiment look extra cool push the rest of the pens and pencils you have through your bag. You shouldn't lose more than a couple of drops of water!

What's going on?

If you haven't started yet make sure to ask a child (or an adult!) what's going to happen when you push the first pen through the bag. Almost everyone thinks that the bag is sure to leak!

You now know that it doesn't but why not? Well, what happens when you take the pens out? (You might want to stand over a sink for this bit!) As soon as you remove the pens you create a space and the water comes out. But with the pens still in there's no room for the water to squeeze out as the plastic sandwich bag stretches around the pens, forming a tight seal!

More Fun Please - Experiment like a real scientist!

- Is it just pens that this will work for? How about pencils? Scissors? Chopsticks?
- What difference does putting more or less water in the bag make?
- Does it matter if your sandwich bag is open or closed?

Don't Let The Fun Stop!

I hope you loved the book but let's keep the fun going!

Claim your FREE digital copy of "Don't Eat Your Slime" - it's 5 star reviewed on Amazon & packed full of more awesome experiments but you can grab your copy FREE at:

www.DontEatYourSlime.co.uk

Need A Unique Kids Party?

Thanks for reading! We'd love to share even more awesome science! Discover why the Sublime Science Party is Award-Winning and how it could make your child's next birthday unforgettable at:

www.SublimeScience.com